How to Survive in Antarctica

How to Survive in Antarctica

written and photographed by

Lucy Jane Bledsoe

HOLIDAY HOUSE / NEW YORK

For John and Helen Bledsoe

Maps and interior illustrations by Heather Saunders

Text and photographs copyright © 2006 by Lucy Jane Bledsoe
Printed in the United States of America
www.holidayhouse.com
First Edition
1   3   5   7   9   10   8   6   4   2

Library of Congress Cataloging-in-Publication Data
Bledsoe, Lucy Jane.
How to survive in Antarctica / Lucy Jane Bledsoe.— 1st ed.
p. cm.
ISBN 0-8234-1890-1 (hardcover)
1. Bledsoe, Lucy Jane—Travel—Antarctica—Juvenile
literature. 2. Women adventurers—Travel—Antarctica—
Juvenile literature. 3. Antarctica—Description and travel—
Juvenile literature. I. Title.
G863.B59 2005
919.8'904—dc22
[B]
2004060639

ISBN-13: 978-0-8234-1890-9
ISBN-10: 0-8234-1890-1

Acknowledgments

I want to extend a big thank-you to the National Science Foundation for sponsoring the Antarctic Artists and Writers Program, and especially to Guy Guthridge, the longtime program director. Elaine Hood and John Evans, of the United States Antarctic Program, both provided cheer and superb logistical assistance. For help with the application, thank you to Karen Baker, Jane Fisher, Sheri Krams, Gretchen Legler, Frank Lucian, Olivia Martinez, and Craig Southard. A particularly big thank-you goes to my editor, Regina Griffin.

While on the Ice, so many people went out of their way to help make my adventures possible, safe, and exciting. Thank you to all the folks at Palmer Station, including Heidi Geisz, Dan Martin, Lauren Rogers, Karie Sines, Cara Sucher, Mary Turnipseed, Maria Vernet, Alan Worth, and Wendy Kozlowski. Thank you to the James Ross Island paleontologists, including Dr. Judd Case, Dr. Jim Martin, and Melissa Rider. In the McMurdo Sound area, I am especially grateful to Dr. David Ainley, Anne Binninger, Michelle Hester, Dr. Berry Lyons, Peggy Malloy, Dr. Dave Marchant, Hannah Nevins, Robbie Score, Raie Spain, Dr. Brian Stewart, Jules Uberuaga, and Commander Stephen M. Wheeler. At the South Pole, Dr. Nils Halverson and Michael Solarz provided excellent informational assistance. And finally, I may never have gotten home again from my second trip without the courageous crew of the *Laurence M. Gould,* who got through the ice to get us off James Ross Island: Thank you Captain Michael Terminel, First Mate James Bellanger, Second Mate Jesse Gann, and Third Mate Jere St. Angelo.

Contents

The Adventure: Why I Went to Antarctica

I love wild places. *Really* wild places. That's why, whenever I thought about Antarctica, my heart seemed to beat faster. My feet grew cold, as if I were standing on a glacier rather than in sunny California. I dreamed about making eye contact with seals and penguins.

When I learned that the National Science Foundation had a special program for sending artists and writers to Antarctica, I applied. That's how I ended up on an air force plane, headed to the far south. For ten weeks I lived with scientists on the edge of the continent, at the South Pole, in field camps next to penguin colonies, and in the mountains. Antarctica was even more awesome—*much* more awesome—than I thought it would be.

So I went back! On my second trip, I took a ship across the southern sea to the American station on the peninsula where biologists study seabirds, krill, and seawater chemistry. From there, I went with a group of paleontologists to a remote island to camp for four weeks and search for fossils. That trip was just as awesome as the first one. In fact, it was so great, I went back *again*. On my third trip, I traveled with an Australian group on a Russian ship. You can bet I'll be going back another time.

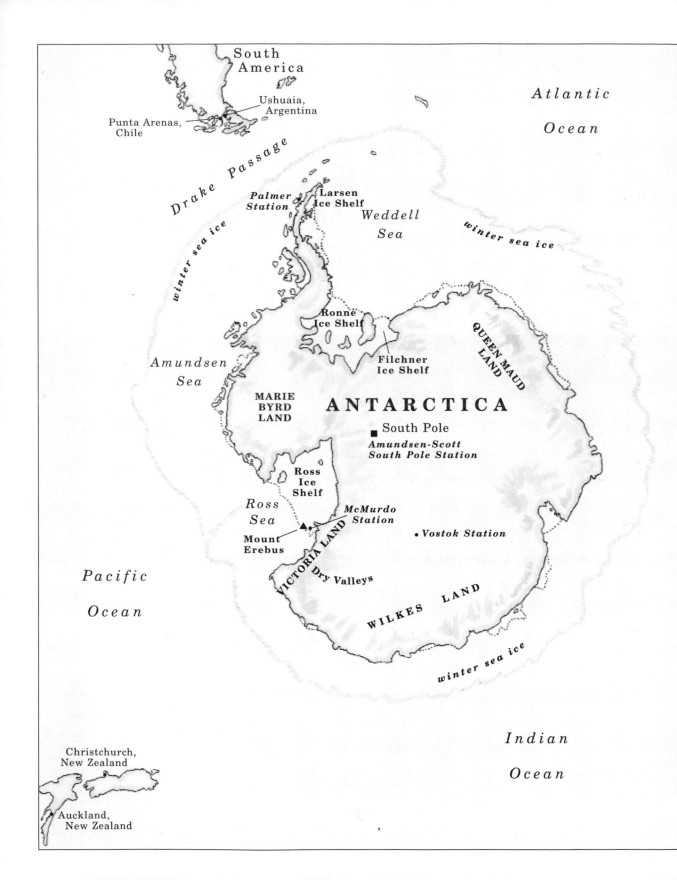

Planning Your Trip to Antarctica

Why would *anyone* go to Antarctica? It's the coldest, windiest, driest, and most remote continent on Earth. Winds coming from the South Pole can howl across the ice at 200 miles an hour. The temperature can drop to 100 degrees *below* zero Fahrenheit (-73° C). An ice sheet, three miles thick in places, covers 98 percent of the continent, giving it the nickname the Ice. There are only two ways to get there: by plane, which, if it flies into a blizzard, might not be able to land; or by ship across the roughest seas on Earth.

If you're the kind of person who says, "Yeah! Sign me up!" when you read those kinds of facts, then Antarctica is the continent for you.

When to Go

The seasons in the southern hemisphere are the opposite of those in the northern hemisphere. Summertime in Antarctica is November, December, and January. Wintertime is June, July, and August. In an Antarctic summer, the sun never sets. In an Antarctic winter, the sun never rises.

For much of the year, Antarctica is surrounded by ice. In the dead of winter, the sea ice forms a huge skirt around the continent, 30 to 900 miles wide and 10 feet thick. This means that Antarctica doubles in size each winter. Only a handful of scientists and their staffs stay there during these dark, frigid winter months.

The best time to visit is the summer. In November, the pack ice begins to break up and the penguins start courting and mating. In December and January, their chicks hatch. In February, the whales are at their most active, and the penguin chicks leave the nests.

Antarctic Challenge: National Science Foundation

For many years, the U.S. Navy was in charge of all American operations in Antarctica. Operation Deep Freeze was the unclassified code name given to the navy's research efforts there. Since the end of the twentieth century, the National Science Foundation (NSF)—a federal agency that promotes science—has taken over, coordinating scientific explorations in Antarctica. The NSF hires an outside contractor to oversee most of the support operations, such as food service, construction, and managing waste.

How to Get There

A ntarctica is very hard to get to because it sits all alone at the bottom of the world. It's more than 2,800 miles from Africa, 2,000 from Australia, 650 from South America, and 8,850 from New York.

— 3 —

Almost all tourists go to Antarctica by ship. There is one flight company that takes private parties to the Ice, but these flights cost many thousands—sometimes even hundreds of thousands—of dollars. They're used only by very wealthy tourists or by explorers who have spent years raising money to support their expeditions.

Tourist ships leave from the port town Ushuaia, on the southern tip of Argentina. Two National Science Foundation ships, the *Laurence M. Gould* and the *Nathaniel B. Palmer,* leave from another port town, Punta Arenas, in Chile. These ships usually go to the

Antarctic People: Brad Range

Each year the National Science Foundation selects a Boy Scout or a Girl Scout to travel to Antarctica as a special visitor. The scout, who must be at least 18 years old, stays for a couple of months and works on a variety of science projects. Over the 2003–2004 season, Boy Scout Brad Range worked on the Ice, studying everything from penguins to ozone levels in the atmosphere. For New Year's Eve, Range was at the South Pole, where he got recruited to be lead singer in the local rock group El Hot Soup. Accompanied by the head chef on bass and a shop mechanic on electric guitar, Range helped the Polies—as people at South Pole Station call themselves—celebrate the New Year.

The Laurence M. Gould *is one of the National Science Foundation's research vessels.*

Antarctic Peninsula, a long arm that reaches out from the continent. To get from the tip of South America to the tip of the Antarctic Peninsula, a ship must cross the Drake Passage—legendary for its stormy weather and giant waves. Many people spend the entire voyage being seasick. Once in a while, the crossing is calm, and then the ship's crew call that stretch of water Drake Lake.

American scientists and their helpers who are traveling to the interior of Antarctica fly from Christchurch, New Zealand, on U.S. Air Force planes, operated by the 109th Airlift Wing of the New York Air National Guard. These LC-130s are outfitted with skis instead of wheels for landing on the ice runways.

An Air Force LC-130, equipped with skis for landing, transports scientists and workers to Antarctica and back.

The flight from Christchurch to McMurdo Station, the biggest American base in Antarctica, takes eight hours. Boomerang flights—ones that turn around midway—are common. The planes can't carry enough fuel to fly to Antarctica and back again to New Zealand. They must refuel in Antarctica. But when there's a blizzard on the Ice, the pilots can't land to refuel. So at the midway point, the pilot always radios ahead. If there's a chance of a storm, the plane turns around and flies back to New Zealand. One third of all flights headed for Antarctica are forced to turn around midway. This midway point is called the point of no return.

The Adventure: Point of No Return

On my flight from Christchurch, the loadmaster, the man who was in charge of the cargo, invited me to sit up front with the pilot. The view from the cockpit was spectacular. Pancake ice covered the surface of the sea. The sky was a clear blue. As we drew farther and farther south, the lily pads of ice that floated on the sea began to connect. Soon we were flying over solid sea ice, and the loadmaster announced that we'd passed the point of no return. We were going to Antarctica, blizzard or no blizzard. I scanned the horizon for any signs of clouds, the possibility of

Antarctic People: Captain James Cook

In 1773, Captain James Cook became the first person to cross the Antarctic Circle. He'd been sent by the British government to find out if there was a continent near the South Pole. People called this continent *Terra Australis Incognita,* meaning "unknown southern land." Cook circumnavigated all of Antarctica but never did see land. He became convinced that even if there were a continent, no one would ever be able to reach it because of the ice.

an impending storm. I had heard stories of planes careening onto the ice runway, pilots blinded by the snow-choked air.

Instead of clouds, I saw . . . could it be? . . . it was! Mountains! The continent loomed ahead, the snow so pure it glowed purple. I searched the horizon for Mount Erebus, the live volcano that rules Ross Island, where the American community lived.

Antarctic Challenge: Hole in the Ozone

About 7 to 15 miles above Earth, there's a thin layer in the atmosphere called the ozone. This layer protects Earth from harmful ultraviolet radiation from the sun. Too much ultraviolet radiation causes bad sunburn and skin cancer. Unfortunately, human pollution—particularly industrial chemicals such as chlorofluorocarbons—has caused a gaping hole in the ozone layer directly over Antarctica. This hole occurs each spring when air trapped by circulating winds gets exposed to the intense southern sun. According to the National Weather Service, the Antarctic ozone hole has grown up to 11 million square miles in size. This is three times the size of the United States. For this reason, wearing lots of sunscreen is crucial in Antarctica!

The pilot told me to fasten my seat belt. We were approaching our destination. One of his assistants gave me a headset, which I popped over my ears. With these, I could hear the pilot's conversation with his crew. Mainly they chatted about everyday things, like what they had for lunch or when they were scheduled to work again.

After a while, though, the pilot leaned forward and searched ahead with his eyes. "That's the continent, all right," he said, "but where's Mount Erebus?"

"Beats me," said the guy sitting next to him.

"It should be right here. . . ." The pilot looked worried.

Meanwhile, I noticed we were losing altitude. Was it possible that we were lost? We were supposed to land on the ice runway near McMurdo Station. What if we didn't find it? What if we landed somewhere else, somewhere remote, in Antarctica?

The pilot and his crew began chuckling. This was all a joke! They knew exactly where we were. Mount Erebus was straight ahead. It looked as if we were going to land on its flanks. The ice grew closer and closer. And then we touched down.

The Adventure: Shipboard Fire Drill

While traveling to Antarctica on the LAURENCE M. GOULD, I felt a bit woozy from the motion of the ocean, but I was doing better than my cabin mate, who lay in her bunk moaning all day and night. Still, I moved slowly, nibbled soda crackers, and drank lots of water to keep the nausea at bay.

On the morning we entered the Drake Passage, I stepped out of the shower and heard someone pounding on the door to my cabin. I cracked open the door and a woman asked if I had heard the fire bell. No, I hadn't! She told me to report immediately to the ship's lounge.

When I got there, I saw that everyone else on board was already wearing a full-immersion suit! Apparently, I was the only missing person and they'd been looking for me all over the ship.

I clambered into my full-immersion suit, a giant orange jumpsuit that would keep my body both warm and afloat should I end up in the sea. Then we all climbed into the life boats. I sure was glad this was only a drill. After that, I took fast showers and left the bathroom door ajar so that I could hear the fire bell.

What to Pack

Surviving a trip to Antarctica starts with packing. Lots of warm clothes are a must! It's necessary to bring good sunglasses that have 100 percent ultraviolet protection, because not only does the sun shine all day *and* night in the summertime in Antarctica, it also reflects off the snow, making for a very bright world. Glasses frames should be plastic, rather than metal, so they won't freeze to your skin! Snow goggles are a good idea, as is lots of sunscreen, with an SPF of 15 or greater. There's a hole in the ozone, directly over Antarctica, and the sun's rays can damage your skin.

Antarctic Challenge: What *Not* to Pack

Waste management is very tightly controlled in Antarctica. Visitors are asked *not* to bring a number of items. Polystyrene packing, such as the little packing peanuts, is prohibited because it poses a threat to wildlife. Houseplants and nonsterile soil are also prohibited, so that no nonnative species will be introduced to Antarctica. Any hazardous or toxic substances are also banned. Aerosol spray cans—such as those containing deodorant, hair spray, or shaving cream—are highly discouraged. The propellants in some aerosols can deplete the ozone layer, and the cans themselves create a disposal problem.

A camera is essential. Some people put moleskin, fabric that is soft on one side and sticky on the other, on the parts of their camera that touch their face so the camera won't stick to their skin.

People need passports because they're going through other countries, such as Chile or New Zealand. But no one needs much money, because other than a small shop in McMurdo Station, there are no stores in Antarctica.

Believe it or not, you might want to bring some dress-up clothes. The people who live in Antarctica work 10-hour days, six

Workers at McMurdo Station make full use of their rare time off. These fellows won the annual McMurdo Station chili cook-off with their "Burning Butt Barbarian Chili."

days a week. When it's time to play, they play hard. Once a year, someone holds a "beach party." The guests arrive in Hawaiian shirts, leis, flip flops, shorts, or even bathing suits. Lots of people dress up for New Year's Day, too, when there's a big chili cook-off and music festival. People pack costumes and props in anticipation of the fun.

If you travel to the Dry Valleys, a place in the Transantarctic Mountains, you'll need something called a pee bottle. If you're a girl, you'll need a special funnel to go with it. Antarctica is a pristine continent that has not been contaminated by human waste. The scientists

Expedition Packing List

An explorer's packing list would go on for pages, but here are a few general items that explorers need:

- skis, ski boots, poles
- tent
- sleeping bag, heavy duty
- stove, gas, pots
- sled and harness
- shovel
- ice ax and hammer
- rope
- snow anchors
- Leatherman multipurpose tool (includes a knife, pliers, awl, wire cutter, three sizes of screwdrivers, among other tools, all in one handy piece of equipment)
- crampons (spiked plates that attach to the bottoms of boots to help in walking on ice)
- compass
- sewing kit
- duct tape
- epoxy glue
- spare parts for everything
- moist wipes
- toilet paper
- clothing, heavy duty
- food, massive amounts of high-energy kinds
- first-aid kit, extensive

who study there want to keep it that way. So all human waste is shipped back to the United States.

Those who go to Antarctica on an expedition will probably spend at least a year acquiring and organizing their supplies and gear. They'll need a stove, tent, sleds, food, and much, much more.

Tourist Packing List

Clothes

underwear

socks: liners, indoor, and hiking (wool)

long underwear

pajamas

indoor pants

fleece pants

wind pants

indoor sweaters

indoor shirts

warm mittens with liners

hat with visor

fleece hat

neck gaiter

hiking boots

down boots

fleece jacket

heavy down parka

Toiletries

soap

shampoo

hairbrush

toothbrush

toothpaste

floss

lotion

sunscreen

lip balm

medicines

nonaerosol deodorant

towel

wash cloth

Stuff

day pack

camera

camera batteries

film or digital card

binoculars

compass

knife

moleskin

passport

books

sunglasses

water bottle

The Adventure: Making a Pee Funnel

"We're out of pee funnels," the woman in charge of equipment at McMurdo Station told me. She shrugged. People are very resourceful in Antarctica, and they expect you to be, too.

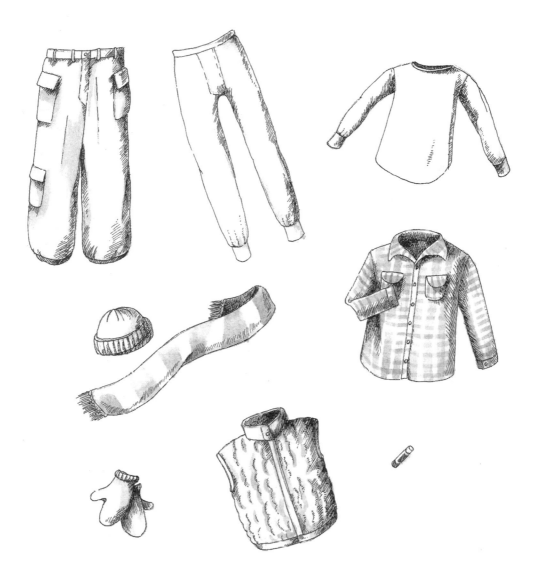

"Uh, okay," I said, panicking.

"Here's what I'd do," she said, coming to my rescue. "Go on over to the carp shop. Ask for an old oil container. You can fashion an excellent pee funnel out of that."

I walked over to the carp shop, which was short for *carpenter shop,* and began pawing through a garbage can.

"Whatcha need?" a big guy in overalls asked me.

"An empty oil jug?"

"Oh. You're making a pee funnel."

Another thing about people in Antarctica: They're very matter-of-fact. There's no time to be shy about bodily functions. He disappeared, and returned a minute later with an empty oil jug. He took a hacksaw and began slicing. "The angle is important," he said. "So it makes a good fit." He handed me the sliced-off container. "Wash that out real good before you use it, now, you hear?"

Where to Stay

You won't find a five-star hotel in Antarctica. In fact, you won't find any hotel at all. Tourists stay on their ships. Even if they are ferried to shore for short visits, they go back at night to sleep on the vessel.

Most scientists and other people who work on the Ice live in dormitories. The rooms are very much like college dorms, and they are shared by two people. A few have private baths, but most have just one shared bathroom per hall.

If you go to Antarctica as an explorer, you will need an expedition tent, one that can withstand very strong winds. You will have to be prepared to spend entire days, maybe even a week, in your tent when the weather kicks up. You will also have to know how to put up the tent—quickly!—with heavy winds blowing.

How to Keep Warm

Forget about building a fire. There are no trees on the entire continent, not a one. The only way to keep warm is to have the proper gear, eat a lot of high-energy food, and drink a lot of water.

Keeping hydrated is particularly important. Antarctica is a desert, and therefore it is very, very dry. In fact, it's drier than Africa's Sahara desert. Most people don't associate cold places with thirst, but the dryness in Antarctica will wick away a body's moisture in no time. And a dehydrated body quickly becomes a cold one.

When a body becomes very cold, a condition called hypothermia sets in. This is when the body loses its ability to warm itself up. Once hypothermia hits, the person just gets colder and colder, and, if there is no intervention, eventually dies. Some signs are slurred speech, uncontrollable shivering, fatigue, and paleness in the extremities.

Once a person has hypothermia, it is critical that he or she be sheltered and given hot beverages and more warm clothing. Noticing very early signs of hypothermia can save a life.

How to Eat

The way to eat in Antarctica is to eat *a lot*. Polar explorers sometimes eat entire sticks of butter, just to get enough calories. Chances are, you won't be pulling a sled for many hours a day, so you might not need to eat that much fat. But you will probably have to eat a lot more than you usually do. Being cold burns up calories fast. In fact, people in Antarctica joke that chocolate is one of the main food groups.

If you go to Antarctica as a worker, you'll eat in the galley, where there is surprisingly good food. The cafeteria-style meals are served four times a day. Midrats—short for *midnight rations*—are served from midnight until two in the morning for workers who get off work late. Because there are all-you-can-eat ice-cream machines and fresh baked goods every day, some people even gain weight while working on the Ice, in spite of all the calories they burn.

What to Wear

Keeping warm in Antarctica requires dressing in layers. For most people, the first layer is long underwear. This can be made of either polypropylene or, for even greater warmth, fleece. Over the long underwear, some people wear a fleece suit, a lot like the snowsuits that children wear. Wind pants and a fleece jacket cover this layer. Finally, a huge down parka tops off the ensemble.

Layers are important for a couple of reasons. For one, air gets trapped between each of the layers. That air is warmed by your body and helps keep you insulated against the cold. Also, sweating is dangerous in very cold places. If you sweat, the sweat will freeze. Then you'll end up much, much colder. If you dress in layers, you can always take a layer off when you feel yourself overheating. Or you can add one if you feel yourself getting too cold.

It's particularly important to pay attention to your extremities—feet, hands, nose, and ears. These are the first to get frostbite. You'll definitely want a wool or fleece hat that covers your ears. To keep the nose warm, most people wear a neck gaiter, which is a tube of material worn around the neck and pulled up over the mouth and nose. You'll want to wear liners under your mittens. People who work in Antarctica are issued a full set of clothing called extreme cold weather (ECW) gear, including all the clothes mentioned above and more.

Keeping warm—but not too warm—is an ongoing dance in Antarctica. It's important always to take the time, whenever you need to make a body temperature adjustment, to just do it, no matter how inconvenient. Getting too cold, or too warm, can be life-threatening.

Antarctic Challenge: Bunny Boots

White rubber inflatable boots, called bunny boots, come with everyone's ECW gear. These are made with two layers of rubber, with an insulating air pocket in between. They're perfectly waterproof and very warm. In fact, some Antarctic workers think they are too warm because their feet sweat in them. They choose to wear extra-thick leather boots instead, so their feet can breathe.

Bunny boots in front of my tent at the foot of Canada Glacier in the Dry Valleys.

How to Build a Snow Shelter

Most likely, you'll have a berth on a ship, a room in a dorm, or a heavy-duty tent to house you in Antarctica. But in case of an emergency, knowing how to make a quick shelter is an essential survival skill.

The beauty of snow caves is that they are very warm. No matter how cold the air gets, snow is always 32 degrees Fahrenheit above zero (0° C), so a snow cave is always at least that warm. In a good, tightly constructed snow cave, a person's body heat can warm it up even more.

There are many kinds of snow shelters. Some are more elaborate than others. Below are instructions for building two very easy kinds. For the first one, you will need only a shovel. For the second, you will need a shovel and a snow saw.

The Mound

Step 1: Throw all your gear, including duffels, sleep kits, buckets—whatever you have—into a big pile. Be sure to keep your shovel out!

Step 2: Shovel lots of snow onto your pile of gear.

Step 3: When your gear is completely buried, climb up on the mound and stamp the snow solid. Then, pile more snow on and stamp it again.

Step 4: Dig a tunnel into your gear. Beginning a few feet away from the mound, dig down and forward, so that the tunnel will come out under your mound of gear.

Step 5: Pull your gear, piece by piece, out of the tunnel.

Step 6: Scoot into the tunnel yourself. There is your snow shelter!

These kinds of shelters are very quick to construct and hold up quite well. However, they don't work if you are one person traveling alone without much gear. In that case, the fastest snow shelter to build is a covered trench.

The Trench

Step 1: Dig a trench in the snow a few feet longer than your height and at least two feet deep.

Step 2: Use a snow saw to cut blocks of snow. The number of blocks you need depends on the size of your trench.

Step 3: Place the blocks of snow across the top of your trench. If possible, create a "cathedral ceiling" by tipping two blocks against each other.

Step 4: Pack snow in all the cracks between the blocks of snow.

Step 5: Place a final block of snow next to the entrance to your trench. Climb in and pull the "door" block as tightly against the entrance as you can. Don't worry if you haven't completely filled in every crack—you need some air vents to breathe!

The Adventure: Happy Camper School

Two days after flying to Antarctica, I stood out on the permanent ice field, an enormous glacier that flows right out over the top of the sea. I wasn't in danger of falling through—the ice is 2,000 feet thick. Even so, the thought of the black sea sloshing around directly below my feet was daunting. Especially since that night I would be sleeping right there, on the permanent ice field.

All newcomers to Antarctica are sent to survival camp, known as Happy Camper School. Our first assignment was to make a snow shelter. In the event that I ever became lost on the Ice, this knowledge could save my life.

With the help of a fellow camper, I constructed a grand den. First we dug a long, deep trench, with steps leading down one end of it. Then, since our shelter had to house two sleepers, we cut body-sized shelves into each side of the trench for sleeping plat-

This is the snow shelter I built and slept in at Happy Camper School.

forms. Finally we cut huge blocks of snow and tipped them against one another, on top of the trench, to form an arched roof. We packed snow in all the cracks. Then I laid out my bed, which consisted of the warmest sleeping bag possible, lined with a thick fleece sleeve, on one of the ice shelves.

After eating as much food as I could stuff into myself, since food is fuel and creates heat in the body, I climbed down the stairs of my snow cave. To get into my shelf bed, I had to lie in the trench, then roll over into my unzipped sleeping bag, and quickly zip it up. Besides the layers of my bed, I wore expedition-weight long underwear and a one-piece fleece suit. I was toasty! Soon, I was sleeping inside a glacier of Antarctica.

How to Sight Wildlife

For many people, the highlight of any trip to Antarctica is the wildlife. You'll want to be prepared to see it all! With binoculars, you can get close-up views of animals you may not see anywhere else on Earth. Most Antarctic wildlife is along the coast. There are three places to look: in the sky, on the ice, and in the ocean.

Look for gigantic albatrosses—with wingspans up to ten feet!—flying high in the sky over ships. The dark bodies of seals and the black backs of penguins make them easy to spot on the white ice. Scan the edges of ice floes for leopard seals. They lurk in the water, sometimes with just their snakelike heads showing, waiting for a penguin to step close to the edge. The Antarctic waters are rich with food for whales in the summertime, and many of them travel from the other end of the Earth to feed in those months. Look for pods of orcas, minkes, and humpback whales.

Spotting Whales

You'd think whales—by far the biggest animals on earth—would be easy to spot. But since they spend most of their time underwater, and we spend *all* of our time above water, meeting whales takes patience and skill. Still, once you learn a few tricks, you'll be an expert at spotting whales.

The easiest way to find whales is to look for their spouts. After being underwater for a period of time, whales surface and spray water out of the blowholes on the tops of their heads. These sprays are called spouts. Oftentimes, wave splash looks like a whale spout. And sometimes, a whale spout looks like wave splash! The spouts of different whales have different shapes, and with practice, you'll learn to tell the difference.

There are two main groups of whales. Baleen whales do not have teeth. Instead, they have baleen, a series of stiff but flexible plates that grow from their upper jaws. The baleen works like a sieve in the whale's mouth. The whale gulps big mouthfuls of seawater, which is swarming with tiny crustaceans called krill. When the whale pushes the water out through the baleen, what's left is a mouthful of nutritious krill.

Minke whales, blue whales, and humpback whales all have baleen. Minkes are relatively small whales and very fast swimmers. Their spouts are "bushy," meaning short and wide. Humpback whales also have bushy spouts. They can be identified by their larger size, long fins, and knobs along their rostrums (snouts). Blue whales are the biggest, growing to 100 feet long and weighing up to 150 tons. They have high, vertical spouts.

The whales that have teeth eat fish and squid. Orcas, sometimes called killer whales, are toothed whales that even eat penguins and seals. Orcas have highly developed social interactions, and they are known to hunt cooperatively with other members of their pod. They are easy to recognize because they are black with white chins, and have big white marks behind their eyes and on their undersides.

Almost There

The trip is planned. You're about to cross mountains and oceans to begin exploring the only continent left on Earth that hasn't been fully explored. One problem: The continent's area is 5,400,000 square miles. That's larger than the United States and Mexico combined. What will you visit? How will you travel around on the ice? Whom will you meet when you get there? Is there a proper etiquette in Antarctica?

The answers to those questions depend on which part of the continent you visit. The following chapters will give you some choices, as well as background on three exciting regions: the Peninsula, McMurdo Sound, and the South Pole.

Put on another layer of sunscreen. Zip up your jacket. Grab your binoculars. Here we go!

The Peninsula

The Antarctic Peninsula is a long arm of land that appears to be reaching for the tip of South America. The peninsula is often referred to as Antarctica's "banana belt," because the weather there is much warmer than it is in the interior. In the summertime, the average temperature is 36°F (2°C) on the peninsula,

An elephant seal rests on Gamage Point, next to Palmer Station.

so it often rains rather than snows. Because of this greater warmth, there is more wildlife around the peninsula than along the inland coastlines.

Palmer Station, an American research base, is located on Anvers Island, just off the tip of the peninsula. There is no airplane landing strip there, so everyone arrives by ship. In fact, there's no real pier for ships to tie up to, so your ship will slide right up next to rocky Gamage Point.

Antarctic People: Nathaniel Palmer

Palmer Station is named after a young American, Nathaniel Palmer, who sailed to Antarctica in 1820. The twenty-one-year-old was on a sealing expedition in his 47-foot ship called *Hero*. Some credit Palmer with being the first person ever to sight Antarctica. However, Captain Bransfield, of Great Britain, and Baron von Bellingshausen, of Russia, both reported sighting the continent earlier in 1820.

The Adventure: Ice Baths

After the LAURENCE M. GOULD dropped me off at Palmer Station, I watched the lines handlers, who were wearing bright orange jackets for visibility and sturdy boots so that they

Two men from Palmer Station jump into the icy sea after the Laurence M. Gould *pulls away from Gamage Point.*

wouldn't slip on the rocks, untie the ropes that held the ship to the rocky point. As the *Gould* pulled away, one crew member came out on deck and sang out a soft mournful yodel. The waves of his voice flowed out over the sea ice. One of the lines handlers, standing on shore, yodeled back. As the ship slipped away, it cleared an open path through the sea ice.

The peacefulness of this scene was soon broken when the lines handlers began stripping off their orange jackets, yanking off their boots, and then taking off all the rest of their clothes. What was going on?

One by one, the men and women—thirteen in all—climbed up on the rocky cliff and dived into the open path of water made by the ship. Some of the divers even did fancy flips before splashing into the icy bath.

I soon learned that the diving was a stunt pulled every time the National Science Foundation ship left the station. Of course the swimmers got out of the water immediately, put on boots, and ran into the station to take hot showers.

Living at Palmer Station

About 44 people live and work at Palmer Station during the summer, and about 20 during the rest of the year. Besides the researchers, there are cooks, mechanics, carpenters, computer technicians, and one doctor.

Palmer Station has two main buildings, Bio Lab and GWR, and several smaller outbuildings. Bio Lab houses dorm rooms, the galley, an aquarium, and of course laboratories for the scientists. GWR, which stands for *Garage, Welfare, and Recreation,* houses snowmobiles, more dorm rooms, a well-equipped gym, and a lounge with a big-screen television, plus an enormous library of videos and DVDs. A boathouse sits next to the water, where a fleet of Zodiacs—inflatable rubber rafts with motors—are tied up. A wooden hot tub squats outside the aquarium, and after a long day's work, Palmer Station workers can soak in hot water while looking out over the sea ice.

Although a chef prepares the meals at Palmer Station, everyone helps to clean up, and sometimes people even volunteer to cook special meals. On Saturday afternoons, everyone at the station par-

Scientists use Zodiacs to travel to islands and to take water samples from different places in the sea.

ticipates in "house mouse," cleaning the station. The station manager puts all the jobs on little pieces of paper, and everyone draws one out of a hat. Other than house mouse, many of the chores are on a volunteer basis, and everyone is very aware of who volunteers—and who doesn't!

A huge glacier is crawling down the mountain right behind the station. Everyone calls the area behind the buildings, and up to the foot of the glacier, the backyard. On their days off, people sled and ski down the glacier. Often people give classes, like salsa dancing, in the evenings.

Residents of Palmer Station have to take boating courses, and once they have, they're allowed to take the Zodiacs out on their days off. There are 13 small islands nearby, most inhabited by penguins, which are great fun to visit.

The Adventure: Camping in the Backyard

The dorm rooms at Palmer are tiny and shared, and some people prefer sleeping in their own tents behind the station. I decided that I wanted to sleep with the penguins, so I began preparations for putting up my tent.

First, I selected a flat site with a view. I could see the glacier in one direction and the sea with its dotting of islands in the other. I couldn't set my tent up right on the snow, because my body heat would melt the snow and make my bed a big bowl. So I found two wooden pallets in a pile of construction garbage and nailed them together. Then I used a strong chain to attach the big platform to the back of a snowmobile. I drove the snowmobile, dragging the platform, to my tent site.

After making sure the pallet was level, I put up my tent on the wooden base. Then I had to make sure my tent wouldn't blow away the next time the wind roared up to 75 miles an hour. So I found nine stones about the size of soccer balls, placed them around my tent, and then tied lines from the tent to the stones.

Each night before falling asleep, I could hear penguins squawking, great chunks of ice falling from the glacier into the sea, and the wing beats of giant petrels flying overhead.

Antarctic Challenge: Blue Whale Diet

The blue whale, the biggest whale species, eats four tons of krill *every day* over the four-month Antarctic summer. Before heading north again in the fall, the blue whale will have eaten about half a billion (500,000,000) krill.

Wildlife at Palmer Station

In the summertime, the constant sun melts the sea ice and produces a thick soup of phytoplankton, or algae. Krill—plentiful, shrimplike zooplankton, most less than an inch in length—eat the algae. Then fish, penguins, and seals eat the krill. In fact, these tiny zooplankton are the main diet for many kinds of huge whales. With these teeming populations of wildlife, Palmer Station is an exciting place for biologists. Most of the research teams study some part of this food chain.

Seabird biologists take Zodiacs out to the nearby islands to count penguins; study the nesting habits of the blue-eyed, long-necked cormorants; and monitor a population of giant petrels. With their enormous wingspans, giant petrels take flight only with the help of the wind. If there isn't any wind, they have a lot of trouble even getting off the ground, although sometimes they can get lift by jumping off a cliff. The bird researchers don't know where the giant petrels go in the winter, but there are hints. For example, guanaco fur in the birds' feces indicates that they've been in South America. Perhaps the most amazing bird in Antarctica is the arctic tern. It flies over 22,000 miles each year from the Arctic to the Antarctic and back.

Antarctic People: Dr. Jeanette Yen

Plankton is the Greek word for "wandering" or "drifter." Phytoplankton are algae, which are tiny plant or plant-like organisms. Zooplankton are tiny animal-like organisms. Plankton have always been thought simply to drift with the ocean currents.

Dr. Jeanette Yen, a professor at Georgia Institute of Technology, studies a kind of zooplankton called copepods. These tiny crustaceans are about the size of grains of rice. Yen collects them off the back of the NSF vessel, the *Laurence M. Gould,* and then sorts through the organisms for specimens to take back to the university for study.

Her research shows that these plankton don't just "drift" or "wander" with the ocean currents, as previously thought. Using chemical clues, they actually hunt for food and mates!

Antarctic Challenge: The Wingless Midge

The extreme cold pretty much prohibits land animals from thriving in Antarctica. In fact, the biggest native land animal is the wingless midge, a half-inch-long insect.

How to Tell Penguins Apart

To be an Antarctic expert, it is essential to know how to tell the different kinds of penguins apart. There are 18 species of penguins, 4 of which live on the continent of Antarctica, while several other species live on the islands around the continent.

All penguins have the same basic coloration: a white belly and black back. This helps to camouflage them from predators. When seen from above, their dark feathers blend with the dark color of the sea; and when seen from below, their white feathers match the ice or light sky above. All penguins have wings, too, but none can fly. They use their wings for swimming.

The names of many species will help you remember them. The *chinstrap* penguin has a thin black line that extends from either side of its black "cap," all the way under its white chin. The *macaroni* penguin gets its name from the line in the song "Yankee Doodle"

Emperor penguin   Chinstrap penguin   Adélie penguin

that goes, "Stuck a feather in his cap and called it macaroni." This penguin has a stylish spiky hairdo on top of its head, with two orange streaks on either side that look like feathers in its cap. The *Adélie* penguin, small with a white ring around its eyes, is named after the wife of a nineteenth-century French explorer. The biggest, most regal penguins are the *emperors,* distinguished by their three-and-a-half-foot height, an orange tinge to their neck feathers, and an orange streak along their beak.

Also regal, the slightly smaller *king* penguins can dive to depths of 800 feet. The *gentoo* penguins can be identified by their white forehead patches. Gentoo penguins are very fast swimmers, having been clocked at over 22 miles an hour.

King penguin   Gentoo penguin

The Adventure: Driving a Zodiac

Doug, the boating coordinator, taught me how to drive a Zodiac. I learned how to steer around icebergs, keeping a distance of at least 50 yards in case one of the bergs suddenly flipped. I also learned how to drive very slowly through brash ice, which is like slush. For the grand finale, Doug put on a full-immersion suit, flung himself overboard, and pretended to be unconscious. As he floated in the Antarctic sea, another student and I had to rescue him. First, I dragged him up next to the boat. Next, I hooked an arm under his armpit, and the other student did the same. We hauled the top half of him onto the lip of the boat. Then I grabbed a leg and hooked it over as well. He was heavy, but working together, we rolled Doug into the boat. Then I took the helm and drove us back to Palmer Station.

Is this seal smiling at the Zodiac or about to bite it?

Antarctic Challenge: Melting Ice

In the spring of 2000, a giant iceberg broke away from Antarctica. The largest floating object in the world, and also the biggest iceberg ever recorded, the monstrous berg was about 183 miles long and 23 miles wide. This is roughly the size of Jamaica. Scientists named it Iceberg B-15.

Most scientists believe that pollution is causing Earth's climate to warm up quickly. This is called global warming. If this climatic trend continues, a warming of the oceans could lead to more frequent and violent storms. It could also lead to glaciers melting at the poles, which in turn would cause a rise in sea level and possible flooding of the coastal areas.

Glaciers do slough off icebergs all the time. Iceberg B-15 may have broken off as a result of natural causes, but it may have broken off as a result of global climate change. No one can know for sure. What almost all scientists do agree upon, however, is that global warming is a serious threat to Earth's ecosystem.

The Adventure: Stuck in Sea Ice

Leaving Palmer Station by ship, I accompanied Judd Case and his team of paleontologists who were going to Vega Island, on the other side of the peninsula, to hunt fossils. After a long and harrowing trip through thick sea ice, Vega Island finally came into view. Our group sent up a celebratory cheer. We were almost to our destination.

But an hour later, we met more bad news. The island was surrounded by an apron, hundreds of yards wide, of fast ice. Soon the first mate was backing and ramming the ship, trying to break through the three-foot-thick slab. The LAURENCE M. GOULD is not technically an icebreaker, and with each forward thrust, the bow rode up on top of the ice, then sat for a moment until gravity pulled it down to break the slab with a loud thump. Each time the ship paused with its snout resting on the ice, I thought the whole ship might topple to one side.

By this time, the ship's captain was stationed in the crow's nest, a high lookout platform, and he ordered the first mate, "As you get in here, if you think you cannot turn the ship around, *do not* continue in. Roger that?"

The first mate rogered that, and we continued backing and ramming, making a few feet an hour, straining our eyes toward Vega Island. As evening drew near, it was finally decided that we couldn't make it, and we turned around. Or tried to. The temperature was dropping, quickly freezing the sea ice against the hull of the ship, making movement in any direction impossible.

We were stuck.

No one thought the trick would really work, but it was worth a try. The crew got out the fire hoses and sprayed the ice cemented against the hull of the ship. It did work! The water melted the ice enough for the ship to move once again.

The paleontologists had to accept the fact that Vega Island was inaccessible. They had to pick another site. In the morning, we got dropped off for a month's stay on James Ross Island.

Dinosaurs in Antarctica

Antarctica is a great place for fossil hunting. The land isn't covered over by cities and hasn't been touched by bulldozers. Any fossils lie undisturbed beneath layers of earth. Of course, the thick covering of snow and ice is a major obstacle in most parts of Antarctica, but the peninsula has some rocky islands that provide easier access to Earth's crust.

In the summer of 2003–2004, Judd Case and his team of paleontologists set up camp on James Ross Island, on the other side of the peninsula from Palmer Station. The age of the rocks on that island matched the time of big reptiles, and he hoped to find some fossils. Mostly he was looking for aquatic reptiles: mosasaurs and plesiosaurs.

Each day the paleontologists fanned out on hillsides, dropped to their hands and knees, and examined every rock in their paths. Enduring the brutal cold, they gathered abundant fossils of clams, crabs, ammonites, barnacles, snails, and nautiloids.

Antarctic Challenge: Bahia Paraiso

On January 28, 1989, an Argentine ship, the *Bahia Paraiso*, stopped in at Palmer Station to pay a visit. The ship was on its way to an Argentine base to deliver supplies and fuel, but it was also carrying a number of tourists. When the resupply ship left Palmer and headed back out to sea, it hit shallow water and ran aground.

For three days, the ship slowly rolled onto its side, spilling approximately 150,000 gallons of oil into the sea. Luckily, the crew at Palmer Station was able to take out the fleet of Zodiacs and rescue all the people. But with all that spilled oil, the birds in the area who depend on the sea to survive didn't fare as well.

Though efforts have been made to clean up the oil, the *Bahia Paraiso* is still there, just two miles from Palmer Station. Its exposed hull is especially impressive at low tide. Shortly after the wreck, divers went down and saw two helicopters on board the ship! Those have since been crushed by the pressure of the water.

Then one day Case struck gold. Well, bone and teeth, actually. He discovered the remains of a theropod, a meat-eating dinosaur. For days the team picked over the site of the discovery, making sure they found every bone fragment. The prize piece was a part of the dinosaur's jaw, with teeth intact.

Antarctic Challenge: Gondwanaland

Wait a minute. How could dinosaurs—giant reptiles—live in icy Antarctica? Scientists think that Antarctica used to be a part of a supercontinent called Gondwanaland, which was situated near Earth's equator. Besides Antarctica, this supercontinent included what we know today as Africa, South America, India, and Australia. About 180 million years ago, Gondwanaland started to break apart, and Antarctica began drifting south and cooling down. This took millions of years. So before Antarctica took its current position in the far south, it probably had a subtropical climate for a long time—a climate perfectly suitable for dinosaurs.

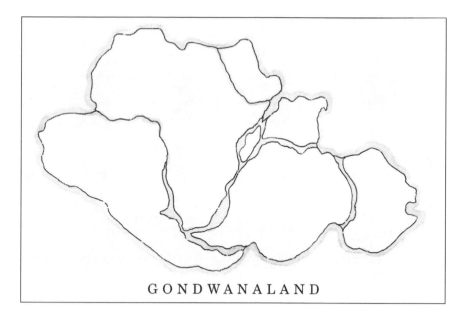

GONDWANALAND

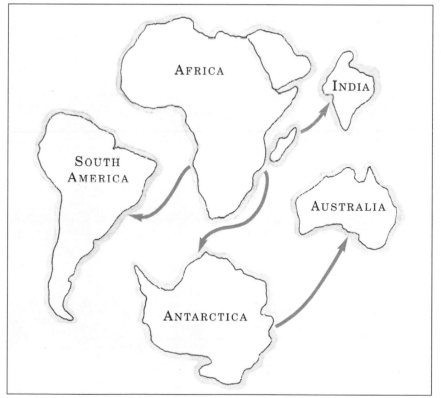

AFRICA

INDIA

SOUTH
AMERICA

AUSTRALIA

ANTARCTICA

McMurdo Sound

If you're like some explorers, you might think you haven't *really* been to Antarctica until you've been on the mainland. Maybe you crave endless ice fields, volcanoes, and mind-numbing temperatures. Or maybe you'd like to arrive by air, avoiding that long, multiday crossing of the southern sea. In that case, you'll want to visit McMurdo Sound.

McMurdo Station is the biggest research base in Antarctica.

Ross Island, composed of four mountains—Mount Bird, Mount Erebus, Mount Terra Nova, and Mount Terror—sits on the western edge of McMurdo Sound. The biggest American research base, McMurdo Station, is located on the island. The New Zealand research station, called Scott Base, is just a little over a mile away. North of McMurdo Station, on another part of Ross Island called Cape Royds, is a big Adélie penguin colony and the site of a long study by seabird biologists. Across McMurdo Sound, in the mountains, are the famous Dry Valleys.

Any visit to this extraordinary area begins with McMurdo Station, the last true frontier outpost on the planet.

Living at McMurdo Station

McMurdo Station is more than a research site—it's a small town, with about 80 buildings and, in the summertime, 1,200 residents. Besides science laboratories, there are a firehouse, a church, a library, a hospital, a bowling alley, and even a greenhouse where fresh vegetables are grown. People who are going nuts from never seeing any plant life can lie in the greenhouse hammock, enjoy the moist warmth, and gaze at the deep red chilies and bright green lettuces.

On New Year's Day each year, there's an all-day outdoor music festival called Icestock. People perform all kinds of music—rock, classical, bluegrass, choral—and just about everybody dances, often wearing their down parkas and insulated boots.

Every New Year's Day at McMurdo Station, a music festival called Icestock is held.

Lots of people hike and ski on their days off. For safety, hikers have to carry a radio and file a "foot plan" at the firehouse before leaving. The foot plan says exactly where they're going and when they'll be back. If they don't check back in on time, a search-and-rescue team will be sent out to look for them.

Avoiding Crevasses

The glaciers around McMurdo are full of crevasses. Luckily for adventurers, safe routes are marked with flags. As long as you never leave a flagged route, you won't fall into a crevasse.

One night four young people went for a walk away from the station. It was getting late, and they had to be at work early in the morning, so they decided to take a shortcut. As they left the flagged route to walk across a field of snow, one girl dropped from sight. Literally.

Antarctic Challenge: Hot Lava on Ice

The 12,448-foot-high Mount Erebus is an active volcano. Steam puffs from its caldera most of the time, and occasionally the volcano spits out red-hot bombs. In 1974 Erebus blew out bombs the size of refrigerators! This volcano is unusual because deep in its inner crater is a bubbling lava lake. Most volcanoes erupt, cool off, and plug themselves up again, but Erebus's lava has remained liquid and visible for as long as scientists have been studying it. Volcanologists have placed video cameras and microphones on the rim of the crater so that they can watch and listen to every burp the mountain makes.

She had fallen into a crevasse that had been hidden by a layer of snow. As the girl fell, she managed to kick her feet into one side of the crevasse and press her back into the other side, thereby stopping her fall. But she was far too deep in the crevasse for her friends to pull her out.

Luckily, they'd brought a radio and called for help. A search-and-rescue team showed up a few minutes later. Using ropes, they hauled her out of the crevasse. Her muscles were exhausted from holding herself up, and she was quite hypothermic. Another few minutes, and she probably would have died.

Getting Supplies to McMurdo Station

The people at McMurdo Station are isolated from the rest of the world. Supplying the station with food and equipment is challenging. During the short summer, Air Force LC-130s bring in mail and food, but they can't carry large loads. Each year, a Coast Guard icebreaker called the *Polar Star* carves a path through the sea ice so that a resupply ship, the *Green Wave,* can make it into McMurdo Station. The *Green Wave* carries machinery, trucks, and large loads of food for the winter. It also takes the year's waste back to the United States to be recycled or disposed of properly.

McMurdo has a small harbor called Winter Quarters Bay, so named because it is the bay where Robert Falcon Scott's ship was iced in during his first trip to Antarctica. If Scott had problems with

Antarctic People: Robert Falcon Scott

In 1901, an Englishman, Robert Falcon Scott, sailed his ship *Discovery* to McMurdo Sound. At that time, no explorer had ever ventured inland from the coast of Antarctica. Scott intended to be the first person to the South Pole. He built a hut, planning on wintering over in it, but the poor design made the shelter drafty. Meanwhile, the sea ice had frozen around the *Discovery*. The expedition members ended up sleeping on the beset ship, since it was warmer than the hut, and using the hut for storage.

The following spring, he and his men, including a junior officer named Ernest Shackleton, set out to see the polar plateau. They traveled for 59 days, getting 300 miles into the interior, farther than anyone ever had gone, but they didn't reach the Pole. As they struggled back toward the hut on Ross Island, Shackleton became quite sick with scurvy, a disease resulting from a lack of vitamin C. He would recover, and Scott and Shackleton both would try again, although in separate expeditions.

The hut from the *Discovery* expedition still stands exactly as it was in Scott's day, just a few hundred yards from McMurdo Station. Because of the extremely cold and dry climate, decay happens very, very slowly. Though over a hundred years have passed, inside the hut some apples sitting in a frying pan on the stove are well preserved.

the *Discovery,* imagine how difficult it must be to dock, load, and unload big modern ships like the *Polar Star* and the *Green Wave.* The Coast Guard has come up with a unique solution to this problem: It built a pier made entirely of ice.

During the winter, workers set up a large rectangular enclosure on top of the sea ice. They pump a layer of water from under the sea ice into this big tray. After the layer of water freezes, they pump in another layer. They keep adding layers of water, and letting them freeze, until there is one huge ice cube. Then, much later, during the summer when the sea ice melts, the big ice cube remains floating. That's the pier! Enormous ships tie up to it, just as they would to a concrete pier. It's strong enough to hold big container trucks that

Antarctic Challenge: The Green Wave

What would happen if for some reason the *Green Wave* couldn't make it through the ice to McMurdo? There is always enough food at the station to feed the community for at least two years. However, if the resupply ship didn't make it one year, the menu might consist of unending thawed hot dogs and instant mashed potatoes.

drive right out onto it to get loads of cargo from the ships. However, the ice pier does weaken over time. A new one is built every few years. There is only one other ice pier in the world, and that one is in Siberia.

Antarctic Challenge: Broken Ice Pier

One year, a huge storm at sea sent giant swells toward McMurdo. These swells surged under the sea ice and cracked the ice pier right in half. The Coast Guard tried to mend the broken pier by pouring water into the crack, hoping it would freeze the two pieces together. That didn't work, so they drove stakes into the ice on either side of the crack, and then wound cable back and forth from one stake to another. In this way, they sewed the crack right up. The solution worked, and the *Green Wave* was unloaded and loaded as usual.

The Adventure: Lines Handler

As a volunteer lines handler, my first job was to keep an eye out for the arrival of the POLAR STAR. When the ship finally slid into Winter Quarters Bay, I put on my ECW gear, ran down the hill to the ice pier, and took my place near the stern. The ship looked huge.

Antarctic Challenge: Antifreeze in Fish

The temperature of the ocean water in Antarctica is below freezing. It doesn't all freeze because of its great volume and salinity. But why don't the fish freeze solid? Dr. Arthur DeVries, who's been carrying out research in the Antarctic for decades, made an amazing discovery: Antarctic fish have antifreeze proteins in their blood!

A Coast Guard captain stood with her arms folded as we waited for a sailor on the ship's deck to pitch out the first line. That line was bigger around than my arm! Since it was much too heavy to catch outright, we'd been trained to stand with our arms extended and to let the line fall over one of our arms.

That part I did fine. After the line landed on the pier, my team pulled it as hard as we could, and then looped it over the cleat. The trick was to not let any of the line fall into the water. A second line was thrown, and we got hold of that one, too.

Then the captain said, "Now dip the line." That meant to slip it under the first line before putting it over the cleat.

I dragged the big line, stepping over the first one, and I dipped it—

"No, Lucy, no!" the captain barked at me. "Get away from there!"

I leaped back from the line. Someone else grabbed it and hooked it over the cleat. I didn't know what I'd done wrong, but I didn't have to wait long to find out.

The captain growled, "What if the ship had surged? That line you stepped over would have popped up. It could have sliced you in half. I've seen it happen."

There is so much to learn about surviving in Antarctica! Listening to other people, and learning from what they know, is the best way to become a good explorer. But making a lot of mistakes is probably unavoidable. In fact, people said "No, Lucy, no!" so many times while I was in Antarctica that a friend made me a plaque that read,

Lucy Bledsoe
GUEST WRITER
McMurdo, Antarctica
"NO, LUCY, NO!"

Weather Hazards

Looking south from McMurdo Station, you can see two islands sitting side by side, Black Island and White Island. If you look directly between them, you're looking due south, the direction from which bad weather arrives. If you see a storm between White and Black Islands, it'll reach McMurdo in twenty minutes.

Antarctic Challenge: Weather Code

Condition 1

Declared when at least one of the following conditions exists:

- Sustained wind speed greater than 55 knots (63 miles per hour)
- Wind chill temperature colder than –100°F (–73°C)
- Visibility less than 100 feet

Condition 2

Declared when at least one of the following conditions exists:

- Sustained wind speed 48 to 55 knots (55 to 63 miles per hour)
- Wind chill temperature –75°F to –100°F (–60°C to –73°C)
- Visibility ¼ mile to 100 feet

Condition 3

Declared when *all* conditions are safer than the criteria for Condition 2.

A weather code is used to monitor safe travel. The worst weather is called a *Condition 1,* involving high wind speeds, very low temperatures, and poor visibility. During a Condition 1, you are not supposed to leave the building you currently occupy.

What would it be like to stand outside in a Condition 1? You probably couldn't stand at all. Katabatic winds—extremely forceful winds that swoop down from the Pole—would knock you over. Also, in a Condition 1 whiteout, so much snow swirls in the air that you can barely see your own feet.

A *Condition 2* means the weather is threatening and everyone should stay in McMurdo Station, but some travel in town is permitted. Ropes are sometimes strung between the buildings for people to use as guides.

A *Condition 3* means the skies are clear and the wind light. Travel is unrestricted.

Different Kinds of Ice

Surviving in Antarctica means understanding ice, and there are many, many different kinds. The two main categories are land ice and sea ice.

Land ice in Antarctica originates in the interior and flows to the continent's edges. As it passes through mountain ranges, it becomes glaciers, or slow-moving rivers of ice. When these glaciers reach the sea, they break off and become icebergs, floating chunks of glacier. Sometimes, though, the glacier flows right over the sea and doesn't break off. This is called an ice shelf. The Ross Ice Shelf, just south of McMurdo Station, is as big as France.

Sea ice forms in stages as fall turns into winter. First, grease ice forms. This looks like its name suggests: greasy slicks of ice on top of the sea. Next comes pancake ice, which also looks like its name suggests: round disks of ice. These grow together and become a solid sheet of ice on top of the ocean, called sea ice. Ice that freezes up

Out on the ice, far away from any open water, one lone penguin leaves its track. Notice the footprints with the tail drag in the center. In the distance, a plume of smoke hovers over Mount Erebus.

against a piece of land, the edge of a continent, or around an island is called fast ice.

In the spring, the ice begins melting again. Ice floes are flat pieces of ice that break free from the sheet of sea ice. Seals and penguins like to rest on ice floes. When the wind pushes ice floes together, they become pack ice, which is nearly impossible for ships to pass through.

Antarctic Challenge: The End of Drought?

Antarctica holds 90 percent of the world's ice, which represents 70 percent of the world's freshwater. Would it be possible to use this freshwater to relieve drought-plagued places like Southern California or parts of Africa? Iceberg B-15 is an enormous chunk of ice that broke away from Antarctica in 2000. If this biggest-ever iceberg could be towed to Los Angeles and somehow stored, it would supply that dry city with water for 1,000 years.

Seals enjoying the ice floes

Antarctic Challenge: Vostok Ice Core

The ice covering the continent of Antarctica is like a history book of Earth's climate. Drilling into the ice, glaciologists pull out ice cores, which can be read a lot like the rings inside a tree trunk. An ice core taken near Russia's Vostok Station is 12,000 feet long and records 420,000 years of climate data! It shows that the current levels of carbon dioxide and methane—two of the gases that cause global warming—are higher now than at any time in almost half a million years.

Transportation on the Ice

Regular vans and pickup trucks are used to transport people and supplies around town. By midsummer the snow has melted in McMurdo, but the streets are very muddy. These vehicles have oversized tires to handle the frozen and muddy terrain.

Sea ice or overland travel is often done on snowmobiles. Crevasses on land and cracks in the sea ice are constant dangers, so commonly traveled routes are explored by search-and-rescue teams and then marked with flags. Near the end of the season, when the sea ice begins to melt, only land travel is allowed.

Snow track-vehicles are used when cargo, or a group of people, needs to be transported. These vehicles are steered using two levers, and like snowmobiles, have tracks rather than wheels. Tracks are wide, ridged moving belts on the bottom of the machines, like those that move bulldozers.

For longer distances, like out to the penguin colony at Cape Royds, or across the sound to the Dry Valleys, helicopters provide transport.

Antarctic People: Jules Uberuaga

Jules Uberuaga works at Williams Airfield, about six miles from McMurdo Station, where the planes land and take off. As a heavy equipment operator, she helps keep the runway clear, among many other tasks. She is also an accomplished mountaineer and sometimes accompanies scientists in the field when they need help. Uberuaga has been working on the Ice for so many years—since 1979—that they've named an Antarctic island after her, Uberuaga Island.

The Adventure: Delta in the Ditch

Having skied out to view the crashed plane PEGASUS, my friends and I were now skiing back. It was a beautiful day, with Mount Erebus puffing steam into the brilliant blue sky. We

Antarctic Challenge: *Pegasus*

Even with every safety precaution followed to the letter, accidents happen in Antarctica. The weather can "go down," meaning it can become drastically worse, in a matter of moments. *Pegasus* is the name of an airplane that crashed in 1970. The plane, a C-121 Super Constellation, had attempted landing in 35-knot (40-mile-per-hour) crosswinds. None of the passengers on board was killed, but the weather was so bad, it took three hours for the rescuers to find the plane and take them to safety. Three hours is a long time in an Antarctic storm!

It's possible to ski from Williams Airfield out to the site of the crash. Much of the airplane is now buried by snow, but you can climb up on one wing and then walk along the spine of the plane.

were getting tired, so we were happy to see the big orange Delta, a truck with giant tires made for polar regions, heave up the road toward us. Joe, the driver, a fireman who worked in New York City part of the year and at McMurdo the other part, asked if we wanted a ride. Rather than climbing inside the Delta, we climbed on top of the cab. Holding on tight, we sang and told jokes as Joe drove us back toward Williams Airfield.

Suddenly, the truck lurched. The top of the cab tilted and I felt myself sliding toward the edge. I braced my rubber boots on the cab roof. The Delta came to a stop, and luckily, so did I.

Joe jumped out of the driver's seat and explained that he had accidentally slipped off the road into deeper snow. We got down from the cab while Joe gunned the engine, trying to muscle the Delta out of the snowbank. The big fat tire just spun in deeper.

We had radios, but Joe didn't want to call for help because his coworkers at the firehouse would never let him hear the end of his having driven off the road. So we took turns trying to shovel the snow away from the tires. Everyone wanted a turn shoveling to stay warm!

Pegasus *went down in 1970, a reminder of how dangerous flying over this continent can be.*

Finally, a few of us insisted on radioing the fire station. Minutes later, a fire truck came racing out on the packed snow road. Poor Joe. His colleagues were hanging out the windows of the fire truck, laughing their heads off about his mistake. Then they towed the Delta out of the ditch.

Wildlife at McMurdo Station

People have no fur, feathers, or thick blubber for warmth. We're slow swimmers and can't fly at all, so getting around is rather awkward, compared to most animals. Our best feature is our big brains—when we use them! Luckily, that's a lot of the time. People survive in Antarctica because we've built warm buildings and

A Weddell seal scratches itself.

designed strong tents. We've invented airplanes, helicopters, and snowmobiles for fast movement. We've also put backup systems in place, such as carrying radios, so that when a piece of equipment, like the Delta truck, breaks down, we can get rescued.

How do the animals that are native to Antarctica manage to survive the harsh climate? Are they better equipped than we are for brutally low temperatures? In the McMurdo Sound area, biologists study the wildlife to find answers to these and other questions.

How to Study Antarctic Seals

Hunting is no longer allowed in the Antarctic, so the seals are not afraid of people. This makes them quite easy to study—when they're on the ice, anyway. The greater challenge for biologists is studying them when they're underwater. Some scientists attach small waterproof video cameras to the seals' foreheads. In this way, they can watch what the seals are watching.

Four kinds of seals live on mainland Antarctica. *Crabeater* seals don't actually eat crabs. They eat krill, filtering it with their teeth much in the way baleen whales filter krill. *Weddell* seals have teeth, which they use to eat fish. Unfortunately for many of the seals, their teeth don't last their whole lives. Because they also use them to gnaw breathing holes in the ice, their teeth eventually wear away. Old Weddell seals that no longer have teeth die of starvation. *Ross* seals are the rarest in Antarctica. Few people get to see them

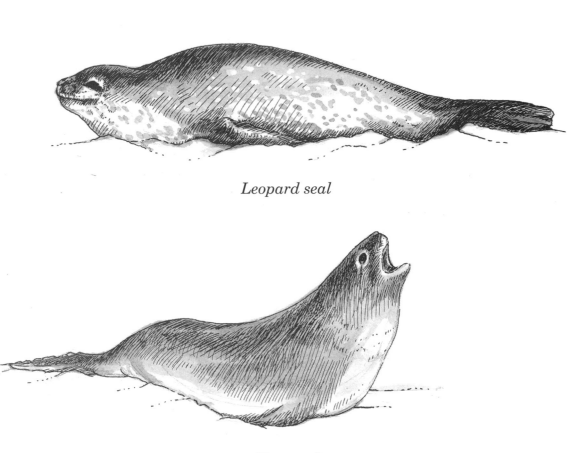

Leopard seal

Ross seal

because they live in the heavy, consolidated pack ice, where most ships can't go. The only way to study Ross seals is to get on an ice-breaker. *Leopard* seals get their name from the spots on their hides. They have snake-like heads and long, sinuous necks. Their backs are often arched, as if they're about to pounce—which they often do. Intense hunters, leopard seals eat penguins and other seals. They have even attacked humans. Luckily, the big, muscular seals hang out on ice floes and stay off land. The best way to study them is from the deck of a boat!

Weddell seal

Crabeater seal

New Zealand biologist Brian Stewart studies Weddell seals. While working, he wears crampons, spiked plates that attach to the soles of his boots, to help him walk on the slick sea ice. He also carries a probe, which he uses to prod the ice before each step. This prevents him from accidentally stepping on a mushy spot and falling into the frigid sea. Early in the season, when the sea ice is solid and thick, he sets up his camp right on the ice. At night, as he lies in his tent, he can hear the seals swimming and vocalizing, right below his bed.

Crampons, spiked metal plates that attach to the soles of boots, are mandatory for walking on sea ice.

Antarctic People: The Seal Vet

"I don't do anything with hooves," says Marilyn Koski, an exotic animal veterinarian, but she's cared for just about every other kind of animal. When she was asked to join a team studying seals in Antarctica, she jumped at the chance.

How does a vet examine a seal in the wild? First, Koski and her helpers put the seal in a net, being very careful to not hurt the animal. She then weighs the seal on a tripod scale, takes fecal and DNA samples, photographs any wounds, records vocalizations, and gives the seal a general examination. The whole process takes about 20 minutes for each seal.

Adélie Penguin Survival Strategies

Some animals have all the luck. Antarctic seals spend hours lolling about on the ice, looking as if they're always on vacation. Humans would die in a few hours if they took a nap—without clothes or a tent—on the ice in Antarctica. Even penguins have to work a lot harder for survival than the seals do.

Thousands of Adélie penguins live on Cape Royds, a rocky piece of land north of McMurdo Station that sticks out into the sea. In the

Cape Royds, a rocky peninsula surrounded by sea ice, provides an ideal site for Adélie penguins to build their nests and give birth to their young.

Male and female Adélie penguins share equally in chick-rearing. They take turns keeping chicks warm on the nest and heading out on the sea ice to find open water to fish.

summertime, they keep very busy maintaining their stone nests. Sometimes they try to steal stones from other penguins' nests, which results in a lot of squawking and wing-flapping.

Once Adélies lay their eggs, the moms and dads take turns keeping them warm. While one parent sits on the egg or eggs—Adélies lay one or two—the other goes fishing. You can see a whole line of penguins leaving the cape, waddling across the sea ice, heading for open water. After eating his or her fill, dad or mom rushes back to the nest. If the eggs have hatched, the parents feed the chicks by regurgitating—a fancy word for throwing up—their food. The chicks eat it right out of the parents' mouths.

Unlike their black-and-white parents, the chicks have a coat of gray down, with black on their heads. They stay snuggled under their parents' bellies for warmth. Eventually, the parents are not able to get enough food fishing only half-time, and they must leave the chicks on their own. This is a vulnerable period for the chicks, as they still have only their soft baby down. For warmth, the chicks all huddle together in what is called a crèche.

Living in colonies, and huddling in crèches, also helps protect the penguins from their worst predators, the skuas. These birds have the curved beaks of hunters, long sharp talons, and wide wingspans that help them soar over the colonies. They prey on the weakest members of the colonies, usually chicks.

Like Weddell seals, the penguins have little fear of humans.

Antarctic Challenge: How to Use the Bucket

The bathroom facilities in most field camps are quite primitive. At Cape Royds, there's a bucket. Yep, just a bucket sitting in the open air.

So there you are with the wind howling at 30 miles an hour bringing a wind chill of –20°F (–29°C). You're wearing five layers of clothing: long underwear, a fleece jumpsuit, a fleece sweater, wind pants with suspenders, and a down parka. You have at least three big problems. One, getting all those layers of clothes off (the jumpsuit and suspenders are major obstacles). Two, making sure your clothes don't blow away in that wind. Three, not freezing to death. If you're modest, you have a fourth problem: nothing shields the bucket from view of other people and the penguins.

Here's what you do. First, find a few rocks and set them next to the bucket. As you strip off your layers, place them under the rocks so that they don't blow away. Use the bucket *fast*. Get dressed *very fast*. To not get dangerously cold, you need to do all this in ten seconds or less. Good luck.

Think you're finished? Not so fast. All human waste is taken back to the United States so that Antarctica does not get contaminated. So before retreating to the warmth of your tent, you have to carry the bucket over to a big barrel and empty it. It's best to wait for a moment when the wind isn't gusting.

At Cape Royds, seabird biologists use a Polar Haven, outfitted with solar panels, for shelter. The buckets on the left serve as toilets.

Field Camp at Cape Royds

The best way to get to know penguins is to move in with them. That's what penguin researchers do every year. No, they don't sleep on nests of stone—they sleep in tents and cook in a temporary shelter called a Polar Haven—but they do spend most of every day in the penguin colony, counting newborn chicks and observing the birds' behavior.

To study the foraging habits of the Adélies, the researchers attach radio receivers to several penguins. Twice a day, they climb a hill above the cape with their radio antenna. They use this to locate the penguins with the receivers. By knowing where the penguins are at different times of day, the researchers get a better picture of the birds' lives.

The seabird biologists keep all their data on laptop computers, which run using power captured by two solar panels. Since the sun shines 24 hours a day in the summertime, solar energy works very well in Antarctica.

The Adventure: Helicopter Ride

"I'm going to load you hot," the helicopter coordinator shouted into my ear. "That means that when the pilot touches down, he isn't going to shut off the engine. You're just going to climb on."

We were standing on the edge of the helicopter landing pad, near the sea ice, on the outskirts of McMurdo. A National Science Foundation chopper zipped in over the ice, hovered for a moment, and then gracefully landed.

"Let's go!" The helicopter coordinator ran in a crouched position so that the rotary blade wouldn't slice off her head. I followed in the same manner.

Once we were standing next to the helicopter, she shouted more instructions. It was difficult to hear over the whir of the rotary blade and the roar of the engine. She showed me how to stow my duffel bags in the cages on the side of the chopper. Then she opened the helicopter door and told me which handles never

Helicopters transport people to and from field camps close to McMurdo Station, such as the ones at Cape Royds and in the Dry Valleys.

to touch and how to work the complicated seat belts. Next, a helmet was fitted over my head. I plugged in the earphones so that I could talk with the pilot.

The helicopter lifted straight up off the landing pad, and then it zipped out over the frozen sea. The pilot banked the chopper so that I was nearly parallel to the ice. He flew so low that I could see fat Weddell seals lounging by cracks and penguins tobogganing along the ice.

After crossing McMurdo Sound, we headed into the mountains. Enormous glaciers slid down mountain flanks. Wide valleys cradled frozen lakes. We had entered the windswept Dry Valleys.

Ernest Shackleton's hut at Cape Royds is well preserved by the dry, cold climate. The hut's interior is almost untouched.

Antarctic People: Ernest Shackleton

Remember Ernest Shackleton? He was the guy who got scurvy on Robert Falcon Scott's first attempt to reach the South Pole. In fact, Scott sent him back home when the rest of the expedition stayed another year. Frustrated but not defeated, Shackleton got together his own South Pole expedition, using a ship called the *Nimrod*. Scott told him he couldn't use his hut, so Shackleton built his own winter shelter at Cape Royds.

In 1908, he and his team traveled 700 miles from Cape Royds into the interior, coming to within just 97 miles of the South Pole. Shackleton made the decision to turn back at that point because they didn't have enough food.

Shackleton's hut still stands at Cape Royds. Inside you can see a well-stocked kitchen, including canned goods, reindeer-hide sleeping bags, and sledges for man-hauling. The hut has the feeling of having been only recently abandoned, as if the members of the expedition are just out for a few days.

Shackleton is most famous for his *Endurance* expedition of 1914 to 1917. This time his goal was to be the first person to traverse the entire continent, but he never made it to shore. Pack ice trapped and crushed his ship, and the *Endurance* sank. His entire party of 27 lived on the sea ice and in a few whaleboats, drifting north with the pack ice. They eventually landed on Elephant Island, off the tip of the peninsula.

Never willing to give up, Shackleton left most of the men on the island and undertook a 750-mile journey in an open boat, with only the crudest navigation devices, in an attempt to find help at a whaling station on South Georgia Island. After 16 stormy days at sea, they made it to the island, but unfortunately, to the wrong side of it. They had to climb over rugged, glaciered mountains to get to the whaling station. Once he got there, he found a ship to take back to Elephant Island to rescue his team, reaching them just before the beginning of a long hard winter that surely would have killed them.

Shackleton failed at his two biggest expedition goals: reaching the South Pole and traversing Antarctica. Yet many people consider him the greatest Antarctic explorer of all time. The feats he achieved in saving the lives of his men are unmatched. He never once lost a life on his expeditions.

Mummy seals found in the Dry Valleys have been preserved by the extremely dry and cold conditions. Some of them have been there for thousands of years.

Mummy Seals in the Dry Valleys

Across the sound from McMurdo Station is an area known as the Dry Valleys, but they're not really dry. There are several lakes in the Dry Valleys, most of them frozen, but a few remain liquid because of their high salinity. Also, Antarctica's biggest river, the Onyx, is found in the Dry Valleys. The river flows a couple of months each summer when the temperature occasionally rises above freezing and melts some glacier ice. So if they're not dry, why the name Dry Valleys? Strong winds sweep through the area, blowing away any snow that falls, leaving bare rock. The region would be better named the Snow-free Valleys.

Lots of scientists work in the Dry Valleys, and some of them have nicknames. The Stream Team monitors the flow of rivers in Antarctica. The Worm Herders study tiny worms called nematodes.

No one has solved the mystery of the mummy seals. Scattered around the Dry Valleys are the bodies of dead seals, many of which have been lying in their exact positions for thousands of years! Radiocarbon dating of the dead seals is difficult, but they are thought to have died some 3,000 years ago. The climate is so dry and cold that their bodies were instantly mummified. One part of the mystery is how these seals got into the Dry Valleys, so many miles away from the sea, in the first place. Another part of the mystery is that the seals are not Weddell seals, the kind found in the nearest sea. Instead, these mummies are crabeater seals.

4

The South Pole

Is the "warm" Antarctic peninsula too tame for you? Do you find coastal McMurdo Sound overcrowded—too many people, seals, and penguins? Maybe you're determined, like other explorers before you, to stand on the "bottom" of the world. Okay, you asked for it: Let's go to the South Pole.

The South Pole is the southern axis on which Earth spins. It's also the heart of the icy continent, the crown jewel of any trip to Antarctica. Getting there is a bit tricky, however. Traveling from the coast, you have to cross mountains and massive glaciers before reaching the polar plateau. Unless you're an expert skier and experienced explorer, you'll definitely want to fly to the South Pole.

Three South Poles

If you're standing at the South Pole, you can walk in only one direction: north. But there are three South Poles. How can that be?

The *geographic* South Pole is where Earth's axis of rotation intersects the surface. A simple sign marks this spot, but since the ice moves

Antarctic Challenge: An Icy Desert?

The polar plateau is a flat, dry, *very* cold place. The lowest recorded temperature at the Pole was –117°F (–83°C). The highest was 7.5°F (–14°C). So much snow has built up over millions of years that the altitude at the South Pole is as high as most mountains in the Rockies.

Wait. Do all of these facts add up? The ice at the South Pole is 10,000 feet thick! Yet it's the driest continent on Earth. How could that much snow fall on a desert?

The answer is, over a *very* long period of time. While less than an inch of snow a year falls at the Pole, it is so cold that the snow never melts. Over many centuries, even millennia, the snow has been building up.

about 10 yards a year, the sign has to be moved at the beginning of each season. In fact, South Pole Station was originally about 400 yards from the geographic South Pole, but because of the moving ice, it may eventually slide directly over the Pole.

A few yards away from the geographic South Pole is the *ceremonial* South Pole, marked by a red-and-white-striped barber pole, topped with a mirror ball. This marker is surrounded by the flags of some of the nations that have signed the Antarctic Treaty. The ceremonial South Pole is used mainly for photo opportunities.

Finally, there's the *magnetic* South Pole. Earth has an iron core that makes the planet into a giant magnet. The magnetic South Pole is the point toward which the tail end of a compass needle points. In 2001, the magnetic South Pole lay far out to sea at latitude 65°S and longitude 139°E. Because of electric currents and the rolling motion of Earth's liquid iron core, the magnetic pole travels northwest about 6 to 10 miles each year.

The ceremonial South Pole sports a barber pole and mirror ball, as well as the flags of some Antarctic Treaty nations. On the right side of the picture is a snow replica of a sculpture on Easter Island. Just to the right of the snow sculpture is the sign marking the geographic South Pole.

The big silver dome at the South Pole is getting buried by blowing snow.

Amundsen-Scott South Pole Station

The research station at the South Pole, called the Amundsen-Scott South Pole Station, was built by Americans. For years, a silver geodesic dome, 164 feet in diameter and 56 feet high at its apex, has covered most of the buildings at the Pole. But the dome is slowly getting buried by drifting snow, so a new station has been built on stilts. It is hoped that the stilts will allow the snow to blow right under the new station's buildings.

Besides the dome and the new station, there are some temporary shelters called Summer Camp, which serve both as emergency facilities and overflow housing during the busy summer months, when 200 people work at the Pole. Only about 25 to 50 people winter over. During these long, dark months, the community at the South Pole has to be completely self-reliant, because no airplanes can land in the extreme cold.

Antarctic Challenge: The Antarctic Treaty

In 1959, 12 countries signed an agreement called the Antarctic Treaty. In this document, they agreed that no country could claim the continent, that it would be used only for peaceful purposes, that no nuclear explosions or radioactive waste would be allowed, and that all countries would work cooperatively for scientific knowledge. By 2005, forty-five nations, representing two-thirds of the world's human population, had signed the Antarctic Treaty.

Antarctic Challenge: Race to the Pole

At the beginning of the 20th century, no one had ever been to the South Pole. In 1911, two men were determined to be the first. Robert Falcon Scott, who'd already tried once, set out from Ross Island. A Norwegian explorer, Roald Amundsen, launched his expedition from the Bay of Whales. The race to the Pole was on!

Amundsen took a team of expert skiers and dog handlers. Scott, too, took dogs, as well as ponies. However, the ponies were poorly suited to the Antarctic, and he had to shoot them. His men didn't know how to handle the dogs, so the dogs were sent back with some of the men. Scott's team ended up pulling the sleds themselves all the way to the Pole. Amundsen's team, on the other hand, passed many of the miles riding on the dog-pulled sleds.

On December 14, 1911, Roald Amundsen won the race to the South Pole. Scott's team arrived a few weeks later, only to find a tent with a note inside saying that he'd been beaten. As if that weren't bad enough, Scott's expedition ran out of food on the way back to Ross Island, 11 miles from a food cache. Too weak to go that relatively short distance, the men died, and their frozen bodies were found eight months later.

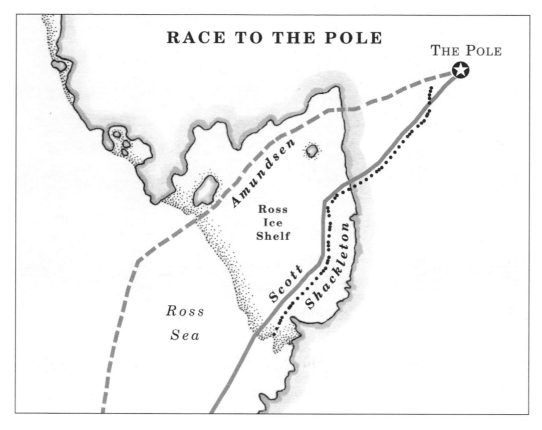

RACE TO THE POLE

THE POLE

Amundsen

Ross
Ice
Shelf

Scott

Shackleton

Ross
Sea

Astrophysics in the Dark Sector

The Dark Sector is a small cluster of buildings a half mile from South Pole Station. In this case, *dark* means no interference from any kind of noise or radiation. This is where astrophysicists do their sensitive probing of the universe, and they need to keep the atmosphere as "pure" as possible.

The South Pole is an excellent place for astrophysics because of the high elevation, dry atmosphere, low sky temperature, and long

This recent Russian expedition drove glacier buggies—so light they could roll right over humans without harming them—from the edge of the continent to the Pole.

periods of clear weather. Astrophysicists have built a telescope at the South Pole that can detect energy, called cosmic microwave radiation, that comes from the beginning of the universe. Data from this energy helps them calculate when the Big Bang may have happened, as well as when stars and galaxies may have started to form.

Wildlife at the South Pole

he only wildlife you'll see at the South Pole are the people working there. The extremes of cold, flatness, and dryness can make some people kind of crazy.

To celebrate having completed their glacier buggy expedition, the Russians launched a hot-air balloon at the South Pole.

For instance, every year a few people try to become members of an exclusive organization called the 300 Club. Here's what you have to do to join: First, wait for a day when the temperature is −100°F (−73°C), which happens only very occasionally in the winter. Then heat the sauna (yes, there's a sauna at the South Pole) to +200°F (93°C—that's almost boiling) and get in it. Sit there until you can't stand the heat any longer. Then jump out of the sauna, run out the door of the South Pole dome, and head directly for the geographic South Pole, several yards away. You have to do all of this stark naked, except for socks and sneakers and maybe a hat and face mask. Most people who attempt this initiation rite don't make it.

They either choose to never leave the sauna, or they turn around after one step outside. But once in a while, a wild person accomplishes the entire ritual, going from a +200°F sauna to −100°F outside air, a temperature difference of 300 degrees. Though they usually suffer for a couple weeks with frostbite to their lungs, for the rest of their lives they get to claim membership in the 300 Club.

Does that sound a little extreme for you? There are still opportunities for you to join the wildlife at the Pole. Each Christmas Day, there is a Race Around the World. Since all time zones meet at the geographic South Pole, it is possible to go around the whole world in a matter of seconds. The route used in the annual Race Around the World, however, is about two miles. For this event, most participants wear their ECW gear. There are no rules about *how* you do the course: some ski, some take snowmobiles, and some ride homemade bikes. Once, a guy rode on a couch hauled by a tractor!

Besides the people, no plants or animals can survive at the Pole. Occasionally a skua somehow makes its way there, but the bird usually dies because there's nothing for it to eat. No one is sure how it manages the flight.

The Adventure: Hotel South Pole

I wasn't about to make a bid for the 300 Club, but I did want an adventure, so I decided to spend a night alone on the polar plateau. I set off on skis for Hotel South Pole, a tiny plywood hut a little over a mile away from the station. My backpack was filled with survival gear and my radio was tucked inside my parka to

I'm standing on the polar plateau, alone on the bottom of the world.

keep the batteries warm enough to function. I'd received instructions to radio back to the station as soon as I arrived at the hut, so they'd know I was safe.

If you counted wind chill—and I definitely counted it—the temperature was −60°F (−51°C) that day. I wore a fleece neck gaiter pulled up to the bottom of my goggles, and my head and ears were covered with two fleece hats. I skied hard to generate heat.

On the polar plateau, the wind carves permanent waves in the ice called sastrugi, making the snow look like a frozen sea. When the wind whisks a bit of surface snow into the air, each tiny ice crystal glows with an entire rainbow of colors. This magic snow is called diamond dust.

Surfing across the frozen sea on my skis, flying through the diamond dust, I suddenly realized that the silver dome of South Pole Station was no longer visible. I stopped skiing for a moment, looked around at the endless ice, and then skied hard the rest of the way to Hotel South Pole.

The "hotel" is nothing more than a plywood box painted black. The black paint does a phenomenal job of absorbing the 24-hours-a-day sunlight, so inside the hut is quite toasty. I threw my pack on the small cot, filled a pan with snow, and turned on the Coleman stove. Then, while waiting for my tea water to boil, I tried radioing back to the station.

"South Pole Station, South Pole Station, this is Lucy at Hotel South Pole."

No answer.

"South Pole Station, South Pole Station, this is Lucy at Hotel South Pole."

Still no answer. I was completely alone, at the bottom of the world, on a continent that was nothing but ice.

I didn't sleep much that night. Some time in the very early morning, as I dozed on the cot, I felt a shadow cross my face. I opened my eyes and saw a man peering in the window. I jumped out of my sleeping bag, pulled on my ECW gear, and ran out the door. By then, he was already skiing away, a tiny figure in the distance. I figured that the man had been sent to check on me, since I'd never managed to contact the station by radio.

Antarctic People: Ann Bancroft and Liv Arnesen

In the austral summer of 2000–2001, Ann Bancroft of Scandia, Minnesota, and Liv Arnesen of Oslo, Norway, set out to become the first women to traverse the entire continent of Antarctica. They skied, pulling 250-pound sleds harnessed to their waists. They'd also rigged sails to the sleds so that on windy days they could "wind surf" across the continent.

Unfortunately, the weather was unusually calm that year. This would have been great for most expeditions, but Bancroft and Arnesen had planned on using the wind to travel much faster than they could ski. Also, their ride home—a ship that would meet them on the other side of the continent—had to leave by a certain date to avoid getting stuck in the pack ice. So Bancroft and Arnesen had little flexibility in their schedule.

The two women did make it across the entire landmass of Antarctica. But from there, the ice flowed another 600 miles out across the sea. They didn't have time to do this final stretch, and so a plane picked them up.

Technically, according to the customs of exploration, Bancroft and Arnesen didn't complete their transcontinental traverse because they didn't ski that glacier to the sea. And yet, who can say that two women who have skied for 94 days, across 1,717 miles of Antarctic terrain, aren't heroic?

The Adventure: Flying Into the Interior

While South Pole Station is the biggest, it's not the only research station in the interior of the continent. On Christmas Eve, I went with the U.S. Air Force to deliver cargo to a remote place, where only four people lived and worked, called Byrd Camp. The four scientists were so happy to see people that they hugged us all, even though we didn't know them.

The weather "went down," meaning worsened quickly, as the air force crew—all wearing Santa hats—shoved a pallet of cargo out the back end of the plane. Standing beside the plane, the blizzard swirling all around, I could no longer see Byrd Camp a few yards away.

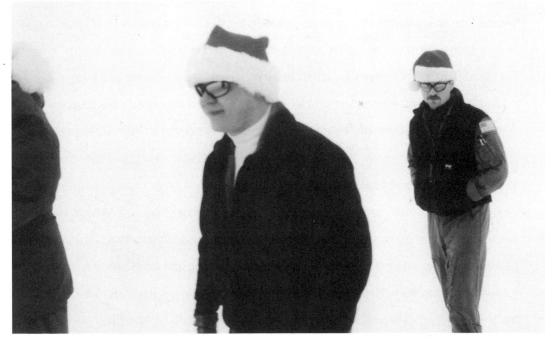

Flying to Byrd Camp on Christmas Eve, the air force crew wore Santa hats.

Antarctic Challenge: North Pole vs. South Pole

Where do you go to see the polar bears at the South Pole? What's the culture of the native people like?

Oops! Antarctica has neither polar bears nor indigenous people. Though the North and South Poles are both very icy places, there are some important differences. The biggest one is that there is a continent under the South Pole, but only ocean under the ice at the North Pole. While the Inuit people are native to the arctic regions, no native people ever lived in Antarctica. Finally, the wildlife is quite different in the two regions. Penguins live only in the far south, while polar bears live only in the far north.

Here's a good way to remember the difference in wildlife. The word *arctic* comes from the Greek word *arktos*, which means "bear." The word *Antarctic* means against or opposite of *arctic*. In other words, no bears!

The pilot wanted to get going before it was too late, so I climbed back on board and strapped myself in. With everyone ready to go, we tried to take off, but the plane wouldn't budge. The skis stuck to the newly fallen snow. The pilot gunned the engine, over and over again, but he couldn't move the plane. Some crew members jumped off and made adjustments to the skis. This helped, and the pilot was able to slide the plane forward. With greater and greater speed, we headed across the snow, ready for takeoff.

This time the nose of the plane wouldn't lift. We slowed down, turned around, and then shot across the ice again, and the pilot tried to get the plane airborne. It wouldn't go. The plane simply wouldn't lift.

Nervously, I reviewed what I'd seen at Byrd Camp: There were a couple of tiny structures, hardly big enough for the four people who lived in them. A scattering of tents—sleeping quarters—surrounded the structures. If we couldn't get off the ground, the air force crew and I would have to wait out the storm here. For how many days did a storm in the interior of Antarctica blow?

Antarctic People: Admiral Richard E. Byrd

The American admiral Richard E. Byrd headed four expeditions to Antarctica. Byrd became famous for using aircraft to explore the continent. On November 29, 1929, he became the first person to fly over the South Pole.

Antarctic Challenge: Lake Vostok

Deep in the interior of Antarctica is the Russian research station called Vostok. Nearby, a huge lake—170 miles long and 30 miles wide—has been discovered! What's more, the entire lake is deep under the ice.

Scientists want to find out what keeps this lake liquid. They also wonder if it supports any forms of life. Europa, one of the planet Jupiter's giant moons, also has liquid seas under its frozen surface. Studying Lake Vostok might provide clues to what exists in Europa's seas.

The alternative wasn't any less scary. If we *did* take off, we would be flying in a storm. How safe was that?

The loadmaster shouted into my ear, "We're going to have to shift the weight, push all the cargo to the back of the plane. If that doesn't work, we may need to strap you back there as well. The front of the plane is too heavy."

Strap me onto a pallet of cargo at the back of the plane? That didn't sound like fun. Luckily, the cargo adjustments worked, and the plane finally lifted into the air. A few harrowing hours later, we landed safely at Williams Airfield at McMurdo Station.

Trip's End

Traveling to Antarctica is a life-changing adventure. No one comes back the same person. You've looked into the intelligent eyes of whales. You've walked on crevassed glaciers and rocky capes only a handful of people have walked on before you. You've learned how to survive in the most extreme climate on Earth. Congratulations! You're now a true Antarctic explorer.

Antarctic Glossary

austral summer: the summer season in the southern hemisphere, approximately October 15 to February 15

austral winter: the winter season in the southern hemisphere, approximately May 15 to September 15

bag drag: checking in for an Antarctic flight, including getting weighed, inspected for proper attire, and handing over bags

beaker: slang for scientist

bergy bits: fragments of broken, floating ice, which often form when an iceberg breaks up

big eye: sleeplessness, often caused by the 24-hour daylight

bunny boots: big, white, inflatable rubber boots that provide complete waterproofing and insulation for warmth

boomerang: a flight that turns around midway and returns to its origin, due to weather or mechanical problems

bridge: the room at the front of a ship where the captain and mates steer and navigate

calving: the process of a chunk of ice breaking free from a glacier and falling into the sea

Cheech: Antarctic slang for Christchurch, New Zealand, the city from which most Antarctic workers deploy

crow's nest: on a ship, the platform for a lookout at or near the top of the mast

deployment: initial passenger transport from airport of departure to Antarctica

DV: *distinguished visitor*

ECW gear: *extreme* *cold* *weather* gear

fast ice: sea ice attached to the shore

floe: a sheet of ice floating freely in the sea

freshies: fresh fruits and vegetables that are available at Antarctic stations only after resupply planes or ships have come in

frostbite: injury to bodily tissues caused by exposure to extreme cold

galley: navy term for dining facility

glaciologist: a scientist who studies glaciers

grease ice: a soupy layer of new ice on top of the sea

growlers: chunks of ice that float low in the water and present a danger to ships because they are hard to see or otherwise detect

helo pad: helicopter landing pad

hoosh (*or* **hooch**): a thick meal that many early explorers ate, made of dried meat and fruit, lard, crumbled biscuits, and boiled water

house mouse: the event in which everyone helps clean up Palmer Station

herbie: a fierce, windy storm

Herc: a Hercules LC-130 cargo plane, which can be equipped with skis as well as wheels, and is used for taking passengers and supplies to Antarctica

Ice, the: a nickname for the continent of Antarctica

ice runway: an airplane runway built right on the sea ice

IGY: the *International Geophysical Year*, which lasted from July 1957 to December 1958

katabatics: extremely strong winds that howl down from the polar plateau to the coasts

LC-130: *see* Herc.

Leatherman multipurpose tool: several tools, including a knife, pliers, awl, wire cutter, and three sizes of screwdrivers, all combined in one handy piece of equipment

lines handler: a person who helps to tie and untie a ship from a pier

man-hauling: using a harness to pull a sled laden with supplies while on skis or walking

medevac: short for *med*ical *evac*uation; to take someone off the continent in a medical emergency

midrats: short for *mid*night *rat*ions; the late meal served for workers who end their shifts after the usual dinner hour

pack ice: the solid cover of ice on the sea formed by floes and bergs being pushed together by wind

pancake ice: rounded pads of young ice

Pegasus: a plane that crashed on the continent, near McMurdo, in 1970

peninsula: an arm of land that projects out into water off a main body of land

Polie: a person who works at South Pole Station

PI: *p*rincipal *i*nvestigator, the lead scientist on a project

rotten ice: old ice that has weakened and is unsafe for traveling on

sastrugi: waves or furrows in the ice made by the wind

skua: a seabird that likes to scavenge food from Antarctic stations; to scavenge or swipe

snow blindness: a very painful inflammation of the eyes, accompanied by loss of sight, caused by too much time looking at the intense glare of sunlight on snow

Winfly: short for *win*ter *fly*-in, referring to the period of time, usually in August, when the first few workers fly in before the main research season

SAR: *s*earch *a*nd *r*escue

Zodiac: an inflatable rubber boat powered by an outboard motor

Historical Time Line

1773: Captain James Cook of the British Royal Navy makes the first recorded crossing of the Antarctic Circle (latitude 66°33').

1820: The Antarctic Peninsula is sighted for the first time in recorded history, independently, by American Nathaniel Palmer, Brit Edward Bransfield, and Russian Fabian Gottlieb von Bellingshausen.

1841: Ross Sea, the Ross Ice Shelf, McMurdo Sound, and Ross Island are first visited and mapped by James Clark Ross, who is trying to reach the magnetic pole.

1901–1904: On the *Discovery* expedition, British Royal Navy captain Robert Falcon Scott explores McMurdo Sound and attempts to penetrate the interior.

1907–1909: On the *Nimrod* expedition, Ernest Shackleton and his team come within 97 miles of the South Pole.

1910–1912: On the *Terra Nova* expedition, Robert Falcon Scott attempts to be the first person to the Pole. He perishes.

1911: Roald Amundsen becomes the first person to reach the South Pole.

1914–1917: On his *Endurance* expedition, Ernest Shackleton attempts to be the first person to traverse the continent.

1929: Admiral Richard E. Byrd makes the first airplane flight over the South Pole.

1946: The U.S. expedition Operation Highjump uses 13 ships to circumnavigate and thoroughly map the entire Antarctic coast.

1956: The American Operation Deep Freeze establishes McMurdo Station in preparation for the International Geophysical Year (IGY).

1957–1958: During the International Geophysical Year, 12 nations establish 60 research stations in Antarctica.

1959: The U.S. Antarctic Program is established.

1961: The Antarctic Treaty goes into effect.

1969: A fossil *Lystrosaurus* is discovered, suggesting that Antarctica and South Africa were connected 230 million years ago.

1991: The fossil of a 25-foot-long dinosaur discovered 350 miles from the South Pole shows that dinosaurs were on every continent.

2000: Balloon-borne instruments launched from Antarctica provide the first detailed images of the early universe.

2001: Ann Bancroft and Liv Arnesen become the first women to traverse Antarctica.

Lucy Jane Bledsoe has traveled to Antarctica three times, twice as part of the National Science Foundation Antarctic Artists and Writers Program. Her many books for children include THE ANTARCTIC SCOOP, TRACKS IN THE SNOW, and COUGAR CANYON, which SCHOOL LIBRARY JOURNAL called "an entertaining adventure story with fast-paced action." She lives in northern California, but can't wait to return to Antarctica yet again. You can find out more by visiting her website at www.lucyjanebledsoe.com.